ONE LAUGH A DAY KEEPS THE BLUES AWAY.

A YEAR'S WORTH OF LAUGHS

A COLLECTION OF JOKES, PUNS, WIT, AND SATIRE

LYN CLARKE

Clarke Books

Anna Maria Island, Florida

Cover design, interior design, and eBook
by Blue Harvest Creative
www.blueharvestcreative.com

Edited by Clarke Books

A Year's Worth Of Laughs
Copyright © 2015 Lyn Clarke

Published by
Clarke Books

ISBN-13: 978-1522754268
ISBN-10: 1522754261

Enjoy the laughs,

Lyn Clarke

Also by Lyn Clarke

Memoirs of a Welshman
Ramblings of a Welshman
Reflections of a Welshman
Amazing States
Echoes In My Mind
The Long and Winding Road
Unusual Wildlife Encounters
Humorous Depictions

Dedication

To jokesters, pranksters and all kinds of
humor seekers, everywhere…
ENJOY THE LAUGHS.

A YEAR'S WORTH
OF LAUGHS

Two elderly ladies were sharing a cocktail. Margaret asked Mary if she would like another but Mary declined saying that she didn't want to be brothelized.

***

A highway patrol police officer observed a man knitting while driving his car. The officer drove up along side of him and yelled "Pull over." The driver replied "Wrong, it's a scarf."

***

I was once at a wedding reception when all the guests began tapping their spoons, on their glasses, to signal for the groom to kiss the bride. The groom looked at his new bride then leaned the other way and planted a huge kiss on his best man's cheek. Yuck!

***

There were two shoe repair shops, in the high street, one owned by a catholic proprietor and the other by a protestant. In an act of one-up-man-ship, the catholic owner put up a sign reading "Cobblers to the Archbishop of Canterbury". The protestant owner, in retaliation, put up a sign "Screw the Pope!"

***

Tom Thumb, Sleeping Beauty and Quasimodo went to a fair ground and decided to see a fortune teller. Tom thumb came out and said "It's a fact. I am the smallest man in the world. Sleeping Beauty came out and said "It's true, I am the most beautiful woman in the world. Quasimodo came out and said "Who the hell is Camilla Parker Bowles?"

***

A woman senior citizen offered her male counterpart "Super sex". The hard of hearing elderly man, after pondering for a while, boldly replied "I'll take the soup."

***

In small town America red neck crimes are the most difficult to solve. This is mainly due to the fact that virtually everyone, in them thar parts, has the same DNA.

***

I once dated a girl from Paducah, West Kentucky and, boy, she really knew how to kiss. When I complimented her, she replied "My Daddy say's I'm the best French kisser in the county." The other strange thing about this was that her name was Ralph.

***

I once had a friend, back in the UK, who thought his future was so bright that he had to wear sunglasses.

***

I bet ten dollars against a man, who was adamant, when he told me that he had walked across the mighty Mississippi River. Apparently, he lived up in Minnesota, near Lake Witaska, where that massive river originates as a stream. I lost that bet.

***

One day, when I was playing poker, I had a great hand but I immediately folded. The hand was two aces and two eights which is known as "The dead man's hand" because it was what Wild Bill Hickock was holding when he was shot in the back and killed. Not so much funny as interesting.

***

A turkey vulture was perch up on a lamp post over looking the a road when he saw another vulture lying there dead. He thought "I guess we do become what we eat."

***

A woman's brassier has two main functions. It is an over the shoulder boulder holder while also acting as an upper decker wabble checker.

***

Some American citizens have a lot to contend with but none more so than the people from the dubious state of Massa Two Shits.

***

A bald man explained to me that he once had a fine head of flowing hair. Unfortunately, over time, it gradually all flowed down the bathroom drain.

***

A dwarf fortune teller was put in jail for false representation. However, he somehow escaped and now the police are looking for a small medium at large.

***

Exhaustipated is the condition which makes you too tired to give a crap.

***

I distrust camels or any other living creature that can go a week without drinking.

***

I once knew a large woman who became a member of a weight watcher's club called The Chubby Checkers.

***

The Lone Ranger has just broken off the partnership with his American Indian side kick, Tonto. He found out that Kemo Sabe means big head.

***

A soccer goal keeper was beaten, all ends up, by a shot, which luckily rebounded off one of the goal posts. He was heard to mutter thanks to "The Father, the Son and the Goalie Post."

***

A pretty young lady asked me to guess what material her new dress was made of. I touched it and immediately answered "Felt." She asked me why I had come up with such a ridiculous deduction and I replied "Because I felt like it."

***

One year, for Halloween, I dressed up as the Tin Man from The Wizard of Oz. All my friends said the resemblance was uncanny.

***

What is red, comes in cans and smells like blue paint? Red paint !

***

At an Italian restaurant the noodles looked somewhat false. On questioning the head waiter he apologized by saying they were impastas.

***

Some over weight people have allowed food to superceded sex, in their mundane existences, and thus are now unable to get into their own pants.

***

I have, more recently, stopped laughing at political jokes because, sadly, far too many of them have been elected into office.

***

The only 4.0 rating, that most University students are destined to achieve, is their alcohol level after partying.

***

The only reason that some people seem to know everything is because they live in their own miniscule world.

***

An old bull and a young bull stood on a hill surveying the cows in a field below. The young bull excitedly said "Let's run down there and get one of those cows." The old bull drolly replied "Let's walk down and get them all."

***

If you have not contacted your mother, for an extended period of time, perhaps a Mama gram may be in order.

***

A young but devoted wife was in the habit of giving her husband boiled eggs every day for breakfast. After several months, of this constant diet, her constipated husband loudly lamented "Eggs again, I'll be bound."

***

Young girls from the age of twelve to nineteen are like Africa, wild and unexplored. From twenty to thirty they are like Australia, highly developed in prominent areas. From thirty one to forty five they are like Europe, mostly interesting. From forty six to sixty they are like Asia, sultry and mysterious. From sixty one onwards they are like Antartica, everyone knows where it is but no-one wants to go there.

***

Two wild berries found themselves being cooked in a sauce pan. The one said to the other "If we weren't discovered in the same bed we wouldn't be in this jam.

***

A small boy burst into his mother's bedroom to find her in a state of undress. "Nice balloons" he blurted out. His mother asked him why he had referred to her body parts with that particular terminology. He replied "Because I saw Dad blowing up the maid's pair yesterday."

***

A Rolls Royce screamed to a halt in front of a run down house. Out stepped a woman dripping in furs and jewelry. She handed a lady five hundred dollars and immediately returned to the car and without a word, roared away. A neighbor woman asked the lady "Who was that?" Her friend replied "That's my daughter who is ruined. I can't understand where it all went wrong."

***

A play boy spent ninety percent of his money on wild parties, loose women, outrageous gambling sprees and endless booze. The rest of it he squandered.

***

In Australia, when a man goes to use the toilet, it is wryly termed as "Pointing Percy at the porcelain."

***

A single young man, an acquaintance of mine, was constantly complaining about his particular set of circumstances of being alone. My invariable reply, to his always annoying plaint, was "Such is one's life in the absence of a wife."

***

It will surprise most people to know that nomads are, in fact, completely insane.

***

I have met some wacky women in my time but the most eccentric and weird, of them all, was a pair of Canadian sisters from Newfoundland. I referred to them as the Goofie Newfies.

***

In Africa there is a seldom seen indigenous tribe called the Oomagoolies. They have short legs and as they run through the tall jagged grass they can be heard to lament "Ooh ma goolies, ooh ma goolies."

***

When growing up I had a friend who constantly referred to John Cougar Mellencamp as John Cougar Water Melon. No amount of correcting would alter his cycle of insanity.

***

No exciting conversation ever began with "I had a glass of water last night."

***

Many years ago an Arab sailor accidentally rammed his boat into a dam. Thus began the annual Islamic religious festival of Rama Dama Ding Dong.

***

I once worked with a man, who was so outlandish and disruptive, that being in his company was like playing chess with a person afflicted by Tourette's Syndrome.

***

After a night out, with his female work colleagues, a naïve man reported to his wife that, on the whole, he had fun. Oops!

***

Two Irishmen were loitering, outside a house of ill repute, when they spotted their priest furtively entering the back door. Pat said to Mick "Isn't that a shame, one of those poor crest fallen girls must have been taken ill."

***

In Tennessee there is an little known law which states that you cannot hang a man with a wooden leg. Apparently, the stipulated method is to use rope.

***

Avoid stepping in soot if you want to reduce your carbon foot print.

***

My mother was a wizard with the old steam iron. In fact you could say that she was very impressive and knew all the wrinkles.

***

If you can't be with the wine you love, love the wine your with.

***

A Muslim spokesman warned the USA that if it did not stop interfering in their affairs, they would send us no more Presidents.

***

It has been so cold this past winter, up in the northern States, that it will probably take until July for the squirrels to thaw out their nuts.

***

Contrary to popular belief, in some parts, Colonel Mustard was not killed by the native tribes at the battle of the Little Big Horn. This mistake is understandable because it was Colonel George Armstrong Custer who was left with mustard on his face.

***

In Olde English, when someone fell over it was termed that he went "Base over apex." This was somewhat more tasteful than saying that he made a total arse of himself.

***

It is said that after a man was shot, outside a casino in Las Vegas, then he staggered inside and cash in his chips.

***

The difference between Martin Luther King and Al Sharpton is that M L K had "A dream" while the other scoundrel always has "A scheme."

***

The Dali Museum has become so popular that, to ensure that you are able to get in, you had better not dilly dally on the way.

***

I was out of town, at a seaside business conference, when I spotted one of my neighbors who was drunk as a skunk. Since I had to drive home that night I took him with me. I rang the door bell at his house when the person, next door, opened his window and said "It's no good ringing, they're all away on vacation at the sea side." Damn!

***

I had a buddy who, every time there was thunder and lightning, he would head for the nearest wine bar. He explained this strange behavior as a case of "Any port in a storm." In sailor drinking terminology, they would say "Down the hatch."

***

I had a friend who was extremely impatient particularly when driving. If a car, in front of him, did not move immediately the traffic light turned green, he would shout out of his window "Which particular shade of green are you bloody waiting for?"

***

When growing up half of our street gang was protestant and the other half was catholic. Us "proddy dogs" would sometimes go to the "cat lick's" late night mass to kill time. We couldn't understand a thing and so, consequentially, we would chant things like "I can play dominoes better than you." or instead of "Amongst women" we would chant "A monk swimming" but it was all good clean fun.

***

A priest, I once knew, fell from grace and was defrocked. I know this for a fact because I dated Grace shortly after him. How he fell off her is still a deep mystery.

***

A girl named Shirley excitedly introduced herself to me. I just could not resist in saying "Surely you jest." Not too original yet an oldie but goodie.

***

A pal of mine was admitted to hospital for an operation. He was given the usual pre-op preparations and the nurse asked him to call her when it was time to evacuate his bowels. Unfortunately it came on so quick it was over before he could advise her. As she approached him, with a stern look on her face, he said "Are you friend or enima?"

***

I once had a pet dog which was a wire haired terrier. Unfortunately it could not bark so I had to get it rewired for sound.

***

I guess the athlete, formerly known as, Bruce Jenner can now participate in the upcoming Olympics Games as a woman competitor. Perhaps he will now donate his balls, to any one of our many politicians, as they all seem to have lost theirs.

***

I once owned a chicken farm but it did not go well. I even tried cross breeding the chickens with spiders so that I could get more legs to sell. The only snag with this ploy was with those extra legs, try as I did, I couldn't catch them.

***

What is the difference between a canoe and a Canuck? A canoe can tip.

***

A duck walks into a drug store and says "I need Chap Stick and put it on my bill."

***

I am told that the name bungalow, a one storied house, came from the building site practice of saying "Bung a low roof on that one." Yet to be corroborated.

***

The word "pub" is synonymous, in Ireland, with "sun screen" because being inside one, over there on a sunny day, prevents a person from being sun burned.

***

Have you noticed that the word sturgeon has an "urge" inside of it?

***

What do you call an irreligious leader of an island nation.? Infidel Castro!

***

When it comes to hiring workers you had better remember that if you pay peanuts all you will inevitably end up with is monkeys.

***

The definition of a Love Child is one conceived on the sperm of the moment.

***

I went to see the doctor because I had a bad case of separation anxiety. As soon as I explained my problem, to him, he yelled out "Next !"

***

Basically, I do not need to be led into temptation. I am well qualified to pursue this sinful endeavor by myself.

***

A Hill Billy explained his simple accounting technique. A1, A2, A3, etc, etc.

***

The thing that I don't understand, about alcohol, is that sometimes one is too many. Where as, at other occasions, twelve is not nearly enough. I kid you not !

***

Understanding the habits of birds can be confusing. By my reckoning vultures should fly in V formation while geese should fly in circles. Go figure.

***

To test the brain power of a boy, who was suspected of being mentally challenged, I asked him "What is the capitol of France?" He answered "F" and you really can't argue with that simplistic, yet logical, brand of deduction.

***

I went to a Pirate's yard sale and to my surprise and amazement they were selling corn for "A buck an ear." Well shiver me timbers and splice the main brace.

***

A distant relative of mine, who had O. C. D, would visit me from time to time. As he was leaving I would inevitably say to him "Don't forget to close the door five times." Just for spite he would do it six or seven times.

***

I know a guy called Stan who, for some unknown reason, must be famous. I say this because he has had several countries named after him. Pakistan, Hindustan, Afghanistan, Kazakhstan, Tajikistan, etc, etc, etc. Must be nice.

***

I have a keen musical ear but playing the piano is not my forte.

***

Unlike his human counterparts the bald eagle has never been tempted to off-set his lack of hair by growing a moustache.

***

I once worked with a guy called Tim Buck. His younger brother was Timbuktu.

***

Yesterday I read, in the news paper, about a shooting that was considered to be race related. Apparently the victim was shot with an athletic starter's pistol.

***

I am considered to be fairly liberal in many of my views but when it comes to my daughter I'm a little less agreeable. Rule one, if you want to date her, GET A JOB.

***

If you ever find yourself having your teeth replaced in Dover, you will now be wearing Delaware dental wear.

***

If your daughter has a boy friend called Paul, who you are not very keen on, just wait a while. Sooner or later you will be a Paul bearer.

***

I was at a card game when a man, who had leprosy, threw his hand in. I folded.

***

The IRS requested me to attend an tax audit concerning my finances. It seems they were somewhat suspicious about me claiming Colonel Saunders, Ronald McDonald and Papa John as my dependants. Picky, picky, picky.

***

I had a soccer playing buddy who, years after he retired from the game, unfortunately lost an eye in an accident. Every time we parted company he would shake my hand and would inevitably say "I'll keep an eye out for you."

***

Where sex is concerned they used to say "Men are from Mars and women are from Venus." The new analogy is "Men are microwaves while women are crock pots."

***

Do you remember that all female musical group called The Spice Girls? I have been told that they had some tidy racks.

***

A man is only as young as the woman he feels. Wow, I think I got that right.

***

I was given some very sage advise when I was a young man. Never smoke and never chew and never go out with dames that do.

***

I don't know if it's the alcohol or not but I think I'll have another drink.

***

Do you remember that popular yet classic musical called "Grease." It starred the charismatic John Revolter with the sexy and explosive Olivia Neutron Bomb.

***

A weary lawyer returned home, late one night, after an extended and complicated trial. He put down his attache and loudly proclaimed "I rest my case."

***

Some politicians are so far left they will never get it right.

***

A Frenchman, from Paris, fell into the river there. This proves, without a doubt, that he was insane. Also the sights, of that city, are sometimes referred to as parasites.

***

An Arab shepherd was caught having sex with one of his flock. He maintained that it was 'Islamb" and therefore he was granted permission.

***

The other day I saw a bird stuck to a tree. It was a fell crow and I hated that sound when they pealed it off the trunk.

***

A pirates toast -- Here's to you and here's to me, I hope we never disagree and if we do, screw you. Aaaagh!

***

I went for a sales job interview. The manager gave me a computer and asked me to sell it to him so I took it and walked out the door. When he phoned me later that day, to return it, I said "Give me two hundred dollars and its yours." I didn't get the job.

***

A distraught woman wailed that she was in distress. To console her I said "It's not the best dress in the world but I can't understand why you are so upset."

***

A man told me that he was from Champagne, Illinois. I'll toast to that!

***

In general the years have been kind to me but how I ever survived, some of those horrendous party weekends, is a complete mystery which I cannot fathom.

***

On the odd occasion some pompous guy will say to me "May I be frank." My standard reply is "Yes, so long as you don't want to be Frank Sinatra."

***

A old retired Air Force pilot was relating , to me, one of his many dog fights during WW II. He said he was attacked from all sides by German Focher fighting planes. I commented that the Focher was a formidable foe in those situations. He ruefully replied "Yes, but these Fochers were Messesrschmitts."

***

As I ponder, about my life style, I often have mixed drinks about my feelings.

***

I have a buddy who is an auto-mechanic and whenever he is ready for an alcoholic binge he invariably says "Get out the toolbox, we're going to get hammered."

***

As a young naive lad, growing up in Wales, one of my favorite pastimes was listening to a ventriloquist on the radio. Doh!

***

VERSE—How's your father? "Alright." How's your mother? "Half tight." How's your sister? "She might." Oompah, oompha, stick it up your jumper.

***

Some people say that Hitler was totally misunderstood because all he ever wanted was peace. A piece of France, a piece of Poland, a piece of Hungary. You get the picture.

***

I suddenly realized, the other day, that I have never been given a lift by an elevator repair or delivery truck. I do believe this could be interpreted as false advertising.

***

This modern electronic age bombards us all with a mass of, quite often, useless and unnecessary information. I feel that to respond to this would be akin to answering the phone during a sexual encounter.

***

I love that song, from the poignant musical Porgy and Bess, "Supper time and the liver is greasy." Ah, the poor man's opera.

***

In England they have a cooked meal which they jokingly refer to as Bubble and Squeak. They say it is so named because of the noises it makes, while in the pan on the stove. However, I think it is so named for the noises a person's body makes after eating it.

***

I recently saw a woman with a cherry tattooed on her lower back. Perhaps this is in response for the one she lost from her lower front.

***

I greatly disliked a particular guy who happened to own the local glue factory. Every time we disagreed I would wish an epoxy upon him.

***

I took my car in for a tune up but it still didn't seem to be running right. I took it back and was told they could not locate the problem as it seemed to be "Lost in Transmission."

***

On a recent trip to Nepal I caught sight of, what seemed to be, an over weight Yeti. I was later informed it was probably the Abdominal Snowman.

***

A friend of mine took over a broom manufacturing company. He immediately announced that he planned to implement sweeping changes.

***

There are two things that the black thorn bush has given us. The Irish shillelagh {walking stick] from its root and the Irish sloe gin from its sap. Both of these, if used indiscriminately, can leave a person stunned.

***

An acquaintance of mine was decidedly the worse for wear when I met him in the bar one night. He told me not to worry as he would "Rise like a pheasant" in the morning.

***

I grew up with a boy called Alan Puddle who married a girl named Marianne Waters. They now have two off springs who are known as the Water-Puddles.

***

Recently I saw a street sign banning street signs. Now that's a typical example of over management by a bureaucracy that's gone entirely mad.

***

I have just realized what that skeleton in my closet is. It is the world hide and seek champion of 1967.

***

In my home town, back in Wales, I recently saw an Asian man giving a highly animated religious sermon at a street corner. Boy, how times have changed because, in days gone by, we used to send missionaries over there.

***

A lot of people died in a tragic fire, in the north of Spain, at a house which only had one door. It is therefore advisable "Not to keep all your Basques in one exit."

***

A long time ago I knew an amorous young man who was sniffing crack before illicit drugs became popular.

***

A elderly man told me that his double hip transplant was successful. My response? Hip, hip hurrah.

***

As a young boy I was so bright my father called me sun.

***

So far as some unemotional people are concerned, "sympathy' is found between "shite and syphilis" in the dictionary.

***

For some unknown reason I seemed to have developed a yen for Japanese food.

***

Some animal parts are simply awful, to eat, while other parts are simply offal.

***

The term that "The fish are biting" has a double meaning. If you are on the shore it is good. However, if you are in the water it is definitely not so good.

***

I once asked a woman if she had ever been married. She replied "Just once but not long enough to cause any permanent damage."

***

My ex girlfriend was a hoarder. I was seriously upset when she ditched me as I was the only thing, in her entire lifetime, that she had ever discarded.

***

I got lucky in my hotel room last night. I do appreciate these pet friendly establishments.

***

An acquaintance of mine recently told me that he was financially flushed. I said to him "It is probably an indication that your life is going down the toilet."

***

My pal's landlord came to his door the other day and said that he was looking for the rent. My pal, being somewhat of a wit, said "Come on in, I'll help you look for it."

***

A plumber named Lee, who was plumbing his girl by the sea. She said stop your plumbing there's someone coming he replied, while still plumbing, " It's me."

***

The difference between the English International soccer team and a tea bag is that the tea bag stays in the cup longer.

***

When it was quoted, in the Bible, that "If a man lies with another man they should be stoned." I don't think it was referring to drugs.

***

POEM—My wife bought a paperback book at the store the other day. When I looked inside her bag, that night, I saw Fifty Shades of Grey.

***

I watched a mischievous old lady bump and grind and thought it could not get grimmer. Then things went from bad to worse when she toppled off her Zimmer.

***

NEWS FLASH !!!! The Cleveland Indians have just hired a new coach. It is hoped that, after an inevitable loss, this 32 seater will get them out of town quicker.

***

I hear that Oxo is coming out with a new product. It is still cube shaped but has a smiley face on it and so it will be marketed as Laughing Stock.

***

Last night I saw a drunk man bumbling, mumbling and stumbling up the road. He looked like he was tore up from the floor up.

***

The definition of a minute depends which side of the toilet door you are on.

***

As a child growing up I was painfully thin. I could hardly cast a shadow, my muscles were like knots in string and people commented that they had seen more meat on a butchers pencil.

***

At my first job I had an absolute ogre for a boss who delighted in hounded me relentlessly. One day I had to remind him that slaves had to be sold, not fired.

***

When people are cremated do they urn that privilege or do they just make an ash of themselves.

***

Two cannibals were eating a clown but one of them thought it tasted funny.

***

A pompous store owner, who sold delicate female under garments, was in the habit of boasting, to all and sundry, that he was big in ladies underwear.

***

VERSE—Let your balls hang low, let them dangle to and fro. You can tie them in a knot or you can tie them in a bow. Ah, those naughty little rugby ditties.

***

I once met a woman who was so intensely over the top, concerning her looks and parties, that her conversations was all about Botox and Detox.

***

Indecisive people should remember that procrastination is the thief of time.

***

A lover's tiff can be described as a speed bumps on the highway of love.

***

Occasionally you might see a couple together and form the opinion that it would be wise for them not to have children. Their rolling of the genetic dice might just suck the sap right out of the family tree.

***

A cannibal asked his friend what was his favorite meal to which he replied "Beans." His friend then asked "What type" to which he said "Human Beings."

***

There exists a term called the Law of Unintended Consequences. A good example of this is when someone shoots a gun up into the air not knowing who the bullet is going to hit when it comes back down. In other words, reckless.

***

A guy called Joe King was in the habit of telling long and uninteresting jokes which usually flopped. At the end of his feeble attempts at humor, I would sarcastically say "You must be joking." He never got it.

***

The rooster struts around the barn yard crying "Cock-a-doodle-do." The hen, on the other hand, sashes around the barn yard crying "Any cock will do."

***

Virginity is like a shot of whisky. There are no half measures.

***

Popeye's favorite little ditty was "I love to go swimming with bow legged women and swim between their knees." Oh, joyous times.

***

Belize is widely considered to be the jewel of the Caribbean. Belize it or not.

***

When singer Jerry Dorsey married a Chinese woman he changed his name to Engleburt Humped the Chink.

***

A one hundred year old lady was being interviewed by the press because she had never visited a doctor in her life. A reporter asked "You've never been bed ridden in all that time?" She replied "Yes and table ended but please don't report that in your paper."

***

A man suspected that his wife was cheating on him. He followed her by car, train and plane, then by hell he copped her.

***

A man told his pal that his girl friend called him a pediophyle. The friend then inquired as to his response at this outrageous accusation. He replied, I said "That's a big word for a fourteen year old."

***

The other day, at my local café, three deaf and mute men came in and sat at the next table to me. After a while their sign language conversation became so intense that I had to politely ask them to keep their rhetoric down.

***

A young man, after breaking with his girl friend, joined the French Foreign Legion. After several months had passed he asked one of the more seasoned soldiers.

"What do we do for sex?" He was told that the local tribesmen brought their camels to town once a year, however, this was to him entirely disagreeable. When the camels finally came, he found himself in the chase. He asked one grizzled old legionaire "Why are we running? The answer came back "You don't want an ugly one, do you?"

***

During a quiz on the male anatomy, a baffled a young girl, after deep thought on one specific question, exclaimed "Oh, that's a hard one." Correct!

***

I don't get it! Peru is teeming with llamas and yet they don't have a Dahli Lama.

***

I still have a slight Welsh accent and when I walked into a store, on visiting England, the female store clerk said "Ooh, you sound just like Tom Jones." As quick as a flash I replied "That's Not Unusual." Boom, boom.

***

At a "greasy spoon" diner, one day, I found hairs in my soup. I told the proprieter that there were gorillas in the bisque. He sarcastically replied "What do you want for two dollars, orang-utans?"

***

A husband, who spent virtually every evening at the local tavern, appeased his wife by telling her that he was now a fully bona fide member of the bar association."

***

A bar tender was so inebriated that, by the end of the night, he rang the bar bell and announced "Last call for incahol."

***

I was extremely shocked to find out, recently, that even monks have dirty habits.

***

In days of yore they frequently used the term "Gilding the lily." In todays jargon that's about the same as putting lipstick on a donkey and that is, basically, futile.

***

A doctor informed his patient that she was pregnant. That's impossible, she said, because I've never had sex. After he explained the facts of life to her she exclaimed "Wait 'til I see that First Aid Instructor, he told me it was artificial respiration."

***

If you drink alcohol, while doing calculus, you run the risk of being issued a summons for drinking and deriving.

***

A plain nurse said to her attractive counterpart "Mr. Jones has New York tattooed on his penis. The pretty nurse said "Yes but it actually is New York Police Department."

***

There was a young girl from Kinsale who offered her body for sale. To be kind to the blind she engraved her behind with detailed instructions in Braille."

***

A friend of mine, whose last name was Evans, lived in an apartment above an undertaker's establishment. We called him Evans above.

***

I am usually a big music fan but all this regae stuff is Jamaican me crazy.

***

When, at a party, a cheeky young man would approach various ladies and say "Tickle your arse with a feather." Because of the loud back ground noise they would ask him to repeat it. Because they were now listenening intently, he would say "Particular nasty weather." The cad!

***

When an American Indian went to a restaurant he would check in, at the reservation desk, by telling them that his last name was War. When a table became available the hostess would loudly announce. "War party of four."

***

VERSE—As the girl scouts would sing around the camp fire "Roll me over in the clover. Roll me over, lay me and do it again."

***

Some men are so barbaric that their brains operate on caveman software. They also have a thin veneer of civilized culture but no moral compass.

***

A young man's dilemma, concerning the opposite sex, is that the brain and the penis are involved in a constant, and intricate game of chess.

***

A girl was taking her cow to be serviced by the bull when she met the vicar who asked why her father couldn't do that, The girl replied "Oh no vicar, that's the bull's job."

***

Some momentous events warrant loud applause but for some of our more recent political decisions, the silence is deafening.

***

During a hotel fire a fireman broke down a bedroom door. There stood a beautiful young girl to whom he said "You're the second pregnant girl that I've saved today. " The girl said that she wasn't pregnant to which he replied "And you're not rescued yet either."

***

Having a conversation with my ex mother-in-law was like listening to the guest speaker at a psychopathic convention. All idle threats and innuendos…

***

Sir Lancelot had a disturbing dream that he woke up in bed cuddling with his horse. However, thank goodness, it was only a nightmare.

***

An American Indian Chief told me that it was he, not Pythagorus, who came up with that famous geometric theorem. Of his three wives the first slept on a sheep skin and had a baby. The second slept on a buffalo skin and also had a baby. The third slept on a hippopotamus skin and had twins. It was then that he realized that the squaw on the hippopotamus was equal to the sum of the two squaws on the other hides.

**

All that I see on television these days is political news and adverts for Viagra. Every day its election, erection, election, erection and either way we're screwed.

**

What does a man stand up to do, a lady sits down to do and a dog cocks one leg to do? No not that, the answer is "shake hands." Quite a conundrum.

**

I was fishing for octopus when I hooked one. To get it onto the boat I asked a friend to grab it by one of its tentacles. In all the confusion he misheard me and grabbed it, instead, by one of its testicles. Ouch !

**

I took my girlfriend, Dinah, to a fire works display. Someone yelled "Can anyone light fireworks." I replied "Dinah might." Everyone ran for cover.

***

I went to the circus especially to see a famous magician named The Great Balls. Now there's a name to conjure with.

***

I met a highly popular young lady who assured me that she was known to every sailor, in the Seventh Fleet, that had passed through her portal.

***

Since my wife now knows everything, using Google has become redundant.

***

I never experience remorse but I sometimes feel bad about not doing so.

***

My upbringing was so extremely tough that it is difficult for me to fathom how I survived. Where I came from it was exclusively blood, sweat and endless beers.

***

A policeman from Liberty Junction had an organ which long ceased to function. He deceived his poor wife, for all of her life, by the dexterous use of his truncheon.

***

In WW II there were many impressive military slogans of encouragement and support but the one that tickled me the most was "Send salami to someone in the Army." That must have made our enemies trembling in their boots.

***

In Hollywood the brides keep the bouquet and throw the groom away.

***

The current political scene has gradually become an Obamanation. Thus the President does not have a legacy to stand on.

***

When I encountered a surly waiter, at an Indian restaurant, I asked "What's the chipatta with you?" To his Italian counterpart I asked "What's the picatta with you?"

***

I watched a long, laborious film, last night, about a guy trying to find a grape that he accidentally dropped on his kitchen floor. It was called "The Grape Escape."

***

A retired old English gentle man thought that his life was in perfect balance. In actual fact this was because he had a huge chip on each shoulder.

***

There are many puzzling terms in the English language like "Opposites attract" which is negated by the phrase "Birds of a feather flock together." Ponder that one.

***

A despondent rural country boy was no good at farming. He couldn't suck seed.

***

Contrary to popular belief not all Optometrists are optimistic.

***

A brain fart is when your train of thought gets derailed.

***

Read on a bottle of wine—A full blooded wine with a hint of acrimony, moral indignation and partisanship. Sign me up!

***

When a woman meets a man she thinks "Your perfect in every way, I love everything about you, now change."

***

Martha was bent over in the garden pulling weeds. Her husband said "My god, Martha your arse is as wide as our grill." That evening he announced that he was feeling amorous and Martha said "If you think I'm getting out this big old grill for that little weener, your sadly mistaken." Boom, boom!

***

Elton John, superstar, he wears frilly knickers and he wears a bra.

***

In my time, I have met quite a few priests who were known to like a toddy for the body. I sarcastically refer to them as cathaholics.

***

A friend of mine worked, in the family business, with his wife and her three sisters. When things were not going well and they were constantly on his back he labeled them "The crochety crotches."

***

Up in Canada, the great white north, it is often very fridged. Consequently, one of their sayings is "It is colder than a witches tit." Then they have the Snow-apocalypse.

***

The three most perpetrated lies are. My cheque's in the mail. In spite of your age, you are still beautiful and I'll put it in a little bit and if you don't like it, I'll take it out.

***

Some vegetarians are such fanatics that they will not eat flesh from any animal, fish or fowl. They also say that they will not eat from any species which previously had a face. This is somewhat puzzling, to me, because they will eat from a head of lettuce.

***

There's a hell of a smell, down in the dell, the gypsies are washing there socks.

***

What do you call an elephant that doesn't matter? Irrelephant!

***

I like the tee-shirt slogan "Beer curing problems one drink at a time." Sign me up!

***

A man, who considered himself to be a budding astrologist, asked me "What is the brightest star in the Universe?" When I gave up he said that it was Cirius. To make light of his revelation I said, in a slightly sarcastic tone, "Are you serious?"

***

A man exited the bathroom and immediately handled some sugar cubes for his tea. His wife, knowing his lax hygiene habits, asked him to use the tongues provided next time. He replied "I have but trying to zip back up is virtually impossible."

***

My cousin was so tight, with money, I swear his arse squeaked when he walked.

***

I once knew a man, who was so down right mean, that he would literally steal the pennies off a dead man's eyes.

***

A woman came into a bar and sat on a stool with her dog next to her. I had to do a double take because, I swear, they had the exact same hair style and color. I couldn't help wondering if she was actually aware of this faux pas as it reminded me of a typical skit from a wacky Groucho Marx movie. Wow, that was scary.

***

Have you ever watched those Latin Americans dancing to that high energy salsa music. I am convinced that they must be hooked on Alka-seltza.

***

I knew a vicariously loose woman named Heidi. I referred to her as Heidi Ho.

***

A mouse discovered an elephant who had fallen into a pit. The elephant offered the mouse anything, that he desired, to help him get out. The mouse worked extremely hard and finally extracted the elephant from his predicament. The elephant was over joyed and asked the mouse what he would like to which he replied "I've always wanted to do an elephant." While the mouse had at it the elephant, while looking for food, bumped a cocoa nut tree causing the nuts to drop and hit him in the head. "Oh! oh! oh!." the elephant cried, to which the mouse yelled "Take it all baby, take it all."

***

Some folks say that "Ignorance is bliss." However, some other people believe that "It can folly to be wise."
Here we go again.

***

An American Indian chief won the lottery and so booked into an expensive Las Vegas hotel. At night he woke up, several times, and asked his squaw to fetch him water. At his last time of asking the squaw came back empty handed and said "No more water. White man sitting on well."

***

When Latin soccer players train there favorite work out is playing Juan on Juan.

***

What is the fundamental difference between a bison and a buffalo? Obviously you can't wash your hands in a buffalo.

***

An irate man walked into an office supply outlet. He said to the shop assistant "I'm not flexible, I want an elastic band and make it snappy."

***

An old man, who was constipated, went to his doctor who asked "Are you doing anything for it?" The old codger replied that he was sitting there for hours. "No, no. Are you taking anything?" The old man said "Yes, the news paper." Next!

***

A new pastor put up his first church notice. "The new mothers will be meeting on Tuesday at 7-00 PM. Any lady wanting to be a new mother, meet me in the vestry at 6-30 PM. Also, next Sunday will be Easter, will those ladies who have eggs, please lay them on the front porch for me to harvest."

***

An elderly man married an attractive young lady and immediately took her away on honey moon. Later that night, in bed, he said that he felt something strange coming over him. His pretty bride replied " That, most probably' is old age creeping up."

***

A constantly down trodden and hen pecked husband finally said to his over bearing wife "OK, I don't care. Beat me, beat me, make me right bad cheques."

***

A huge fire broke out at a circus. As the big top was burning a clown staggered out carrying a nubile, prim and proper young girl. The news paper headline, the next day, read "Virgin On The Ridiculous."

***

At a party I asked if anyone wanted a drink. A woman replied "Might I" so being an obedient kind of guy, that I am, I brought her a Mai Tai.

***

Two young men, who were great pals, went with their brides on honey moon together. They had a bet as to who would have the most sex on their first night. The agreement was that each would leave a note, on the outside of the bedroom door. The first guy had three and so he marked 111. On seeing this the other guy read it as one hundred and eleven, so he left a note saying "You beat me by two."

***

A man and his date drove out into the country side in his aging sports car. On going up a steep hill the car quit. The man said "We'll have to get out and shove it up." To which his girl friend said "Sure but will it be OK to leave the car here."

***

A catholic girl left her rural village and took off for the big city. Years later she returned with abundant riches. A woman asked her mother how she became so wealthy. When the mother replied the neighbor fainted dead away. When she was revived she said "I can't believe your daughter is a protestant."

***

A woman was questioned about her outstanding debts. She explained that it was because she had so many children. The collector indicated that the fault lay between her and her husband. To which she said "Yes, it's sex of one or half dozen of the other."

***

Twins are womb mates who are soon to become bosom buddies.

***

When retirement finally arrives its "Goodbye tension, hello pension."

***

When a man was told that his friend's daughter was getting married he said that he didn't even know that she was pregnant. When told that she was not at all pregnant he replied "Well that's just flaunting middle class snobbery."

***

A mother was assisting her daughter to get dressed on her wedding day. The mother asked, the bride to be, if she had any uncertain reservations about the up coming event. The daughter replied "No, I've never been so cock sure in all my life."

***

An elderly Scottish man told his three sons he would buy them each a gift so long as it was designed with tartan. The first two wanted a tartan hat and a tartan scarf. The third one asked for a hundred pounds because he had put a tart in trouble.

***

An uneducated man's wife became pregnant again. His doctor asked if he had used a sheath as he had instructed. The man said "I read the instructions and it said to stretch it over the organ but because we don't have one, I stretched it over the piano."

***

A Republican woman married a Democrat man. In the middle of their first honey moon night she said "There's a split in the Republican party and if the Democrat member stood now, he would get in easily. The man replied "Too late. I stood as an independent and lost my deposit."

***

In Greek mythology Meduca was known to complain about her bad snake days.

***

I once heard of a man who was an under ground Sewer Manager. He would laboriously describe himself as being a member of the effluent society.

***

EPITAPH. Here lies the remains of Mary Charlotte, a highly respected local harlot. For fourteen years she kept her virginity, a respectful time for this vicinity.

***

A young girl was sent to the doctor with restless leg syndrome. He asked if she was troubled by explicit or erotic dreams. She replied "No, I take them in my stride."

***

A farmer asked his neighbor why his cattle bred so well and his didn't. The neighbor said that the Vet had given him some sex pills to which his friend asked "What's in them." the neighbor said "I don't know but they taste like pepper mint."

***

I met an outstanding woman the other day. She had everything that a virile man could wish for. A beard, moustache, muscles, etc, etc.

***

POEM—There was a young man from Poole, who found a red ring on his tool. The doctor, a cynic, said at the clinic "Don't sweat it, that's lipstick you fool."

***

Everyone, in the current political scene, is anxiously waiting to see if Donald will play his trump card. Perhaps the time is right for a better hair piece.

***

An out of town business man haggled with a call girl over her fee. He offer twenty dollars but she wanted a hundred. The business man declined and later, with his gargoyle of a wife at dinner that night, he was astonished to see the same call girl seated on the next table. She looked at him and said "See, that's what you get for twenty dollars."

***

A rueful man said to his friend "I hope that I get an STD." His friend asked him why and the distraught man replied "Because I can go home and give it to the maid, who will give it to my father, who will give it to my mother, who will give it to the vicar, who will give it to his daughter, who will give it to the head master. That's the rotten beggar I'm after." A trail of human wreckage!

***

A man drove all day and booked into a hotel for a good nights sleep. Alas, he was kept awake, all night, by the noises coming from the hall below his room. He phoned the front desk and asked for an explanation. The night porter explained that they were holding the Policeman's Ball, to which the irate man said "Well, for God's sake let it go."

***

A naïve young lady was late for an important meeting. Her excuse was that on her way, via a narrow cliff top path, she encountered a young man. She said that she didn't know whether to toss him off or let him block my passage.

***

I once worked for an uncompromising boss who would not entertain anyone else's point of view. When it came to work his motto was "It's my way or the highway."

***

As a child I had such a fair complexion that my skin usually burned during summer time and so my mother to slathered me with an ocean of calamine lotion.

***

Seen on an advertising board outside a rural restaurant near Portrush, Northern Ireland. "Soup of the day—Whiskey."

***

Some times I think that I can see the light at the end of the tunnel. However, as I get older the glimmer is getting dimmer.

***

A mistress is someone who comes between a mister and a mattress.

***

When Robin Williams arrived at the Pearly Gates, of that great theater in the sky, he asked Saint Peter "Is there anything available in the front row?"

***

A lady had an obnoxious male parrot which was always saying "I want to poke." Thinking that a female partner would subdue him, she went to the pet store but all they had was a female owl. She brought it home and when the parrot said his usual phrase, the owl went "Oooh, oooh" To which he replied "Not you , you google eyed freak."

***

When Scottish people say the word "mouse" they pronounce it "moose." Which gives a whole new meaning to the term "There's a moose loose aboot the hoose."

***

German people have the commendable traits of being very precise and disciplined. This is all well and good but, without any shadow of a doubt, there jokes are the wurst.

***

In the southern States of America wild hog hunting is an avid sport. It could be described as trying to entice a square pig into a round hole.

***

The star zoo monkey was so upset that he couldn't perform his usual auto-erotic activities. He also was not able to decide which end he should stick his banana.

***

My life's mantra has changed from "Sex, drugs and rock and roll" to "Text, hugs and sausage rolls.

***

When climbing in the Himalayas, at the top of the world, it is so exhausting that it could be described as Nepaling.

***

Mrs. Clinton's bid, to run for the White House is, nothing short of hilarious.

***

A wise man once told me that money has no value until you spend it. For example, if you are marooned on a desert island, a million dollars is worthless.

***

A scheme and a scam are different. In a scheme you can lose a lot of money but in a scam you can lose everything and end up in shite house creek without a paddle.

***

I love that line, in a recent county and western song, "Whisky for my men and beer for the horses."

***

Before going into battle the leader said "Men, I'm afraid that we only have a fifty percent chance." One of his subordinates asked " Which, fifty percent chance of winning or fifty percent chance of losing?"

***

A gentleman is one who hears a lady singing in the bath tub and puts his ear to the key hole.

***

By back to school time my mother's wish list was extra vodka and valium.

***

A friend of mine had a plaster cast removed after breaking his wrist. He said to the doctor "Will I now be able to play the piano? When the doctor said that he would, my friend replied. "That's remarkable because I was not able to play it before."

***

A part time actor was talking to one of his companions and told him that he had been given a small part in "The Grapes of Wrath." When his associate asked which part he replied "Just one of the bunch."

***

A word to the uninitiated. When you see a crazy man going on his merry way just remember one thing. He is just as happy in his world, as you are in yours.

***

It has come to my attention, over recent years, that many girls are wearing various colorful monogrammed apparel. However, no matter what the colors of these garments are, they are invariably embossed with the word "Pink."

***

A well heeled older man walked into a gym and asked the trainer "Which machine would be best, for me to use, in my attempt to meet beautiful younger women?" The trainer looked the unfit man up and down then replied "I recommend the ATM."

***

Back in Wales, when growing up, our streets were so narrow that people couldn't pass each other without someone getting pregnant.

***

VERSE—It wasn't the grass that tickled her arse, it was my finger. It wasn't the breeze that tickled her knees, It was my finger. Aah, poetry at its best.

***

POEM—There once was a wicked old actor who waylaid a young girl and attacked her. In reply to this trick she bit of his wick and thus remained virgo intacta.

***

A man, unwisely, took a snake into a bar. On being told that it was poisonous, the owner asked what needed to be done if it bit anyone. The man said that the poison would have to be sucked out. The owner then asked "What if the bite is in the backside" to which the man replied "That's when you find out who your true friends really are."

***

The boxing champion of the Philippines could, most definitely, Pacquio a punch.

***

An old saying, concerning needy peoples financial plight, is "When the rent collector comes to the door, love flies out the window." Metaphorically this means getting a wake up call.

***

The ugly duckling was truly gruesome. Unfortunately, it grew some more.

***

I hear that NASA is going to put an Expresso machine on the next space shuttle. If nothing else it will ensure that the astronaughts have an all time high.

***

In that classic Hollywood movie *Gone With the Wind*, I thought the male lead role, Rhetoric Butler, was aptly named due to his outrageous southern attitude.

***

A female terrorist bomber tried to enter an exclusive restaurant but she was "re-fused" on the grounds that her burka was not in keeping with their dress code.

***

On a visit, to the UK, I stumbled out of a Fish and Chip shop and bumped into another patron. He apologized but I said "No bother, let the chips fall where they may."

***

Having found a dollar a man put it in his pants pocket which had a hole in it and the coin was immediately lost. Thus the adage "A fool and his money are soon parted."

***

I once met a woman who was gifted with a well endowed figure. Her breast were so ample that, if

69

necessary, she could suckle two sets of twins in one sitting. Ah, the milk of human kindness.

***

There was a young man from Pagoda who wouldn't pay a whore what he owed her. So she jumped out of bed, all flustered and red, and spit in his whisky and soda.

***

A man, all battered and bruised, went to the doctor who asked what had happened. The man said that his wife talked in her sleep and said "Look out my husband is coming." Being still half asleep, I panicked and jumped straight out the window."

***

My wife and I were married, on the beautiful beach, about a hundred yards from our house. It was obviously a low budget affair because we incurred no overheads.

***

If you are in the habit of picking up young ladies, at the bar, you should be aware of the age old saying that "Beauty is in the eye of the beer holder."

***

Is it just me or does anyone else find it ironic that the recent dispute over not issuing marriage licenses to gay couples is occurring in Morehead, Kentucky?

***

A country man, up before the judge for poaching, said that his occupation was a pheasant plucker. The elderly, partially deaf, judge said "You are a clever what?"

***

It is a little known fact but I can assure you that cockles do not transmit pneumo-coccal pneumonia.

***

After a strenuous bout of lifting a young man developed a hernia which rendered his genitalia to sag more than normally required. When he complained, his friend jokingly advised him to spray the affected area with knacker laquer.

***

Recently I accompanied a cute lady to a long and boring opera but in all honesty it was not my cup of tea. I've actually had more fun during a root canal at the dentist.

***

Robin Hood and Little John were walking through a forest. Little John said to Robin "Would you like to give this forest a name?" Robin replied "Sure would."

***

A strumpet of a woman once called me pretentious. I considered this to be outrageous considering she was standing there with painted on make-up, wearing high heeled shoes, sporting an obvious wig and sticking out her store bought boobs.

***

A man was about to give a talk on how best to cross the Alps with elephants. He introduced himself as Proffessor Hannibal Lecture.

***

A Peruvian "Hello" can be described as an incantation.

***

When a missile is approaching and someone yells "Heads up" this is the worse advice that can be given. What they actually mean to relay is "Heads down." because doing the opposite usually entails being hit by some flying object.

***

I hate being told something funny at the exact moment that I am deeply inhaling a sip of coffee. This usually entails me blowing the coffee out of my nose in an entirely undignified manner. In other words, somewhat a little less than graceful.

***

You would think with all the words available, in the English language, that they would be used more susinctly. For example, some people go to the Golf Club to play a game with a golf club. A thought provoking mystery wrapped up in an enigma.

***

At a prestigious dinner an attractive, shapely woman was introduced as the President of the National Bank. She said "No, Mr. Jones is, I am just his vice."

***

I love one line jokes because I find that brevity is the soul of wit.

***

My guilty pleasure is drinking a beer while taking a long cool shower. It conjures up the ambiance of me being the master of my own domain. Oh happy days.

***

I could never date a female vampire because I would rather be smitten than bitten. Hey, once bitten, twice shy.

***

Recently a top General, in the armed forces, was discharged for having classified messages on his personal computer. The query is "Did General Patraeus realy betray us?"

***

I knew a man who was consistently misplacing things but he was never worried about his misdeeds. He could care less about him being careless.

***

I recently watched the Indianapolis 500 on the television. They should probably change the term NASCAR to "Smash Car" because the majority of the drivers never did see the checkered flag.

***

For young men, who have not yet married, please remember a happy wife means a happy life. In other words, if Mama's not happy, noooooo body's happy.

***

Adolescence comes between infancy and adultery.

***

If I was asked to pick a super all star soccer team my first choice would be Jesus as goal keeper. He has saved millions and he looks great on crosses.

***

It has been my pleasure to have met some mighty fine women in my time. I remember one beautiful Polynesian girl who I adored and called her my Honolulu Lulu. Come to think of it, that Yokohama Mama wasn't half bad either.

***

It is widely said that a ducks arse is water tight. This probably explains why their shite comes out looking like something squirted from a tooth paste tube.

***

A pal of mine, without thinking, dived into the ocean without taking his money out of his shorts pocket. He lost about sixty dollars and I have heard of several other similar incidents. I suspect these unsuspected incidents are brought on by a crime wave.

***

Some young men these days, whether they realize it or not, are over hairy what with their long unkempt locks and scraggly beards. I call it the Neanderthal look because, I swear, if they had tusks they would resemble wooly mammoths.

***

Rugby is sometimes refered to as a sport played by men with peculiar balls.

***

When a bear hibernates, for the entire six months of winter, this really is the epitome of the term "The bare necessities."

***

A new State slogan, to attract tourism, is "Come to Utah, give polygamy a try."

***

When a prominent biblical character threatened to bring the ten plagues to decend upon Egypt, the Pharaoh said "For goodness sake Moses, smell the roses."

***

The most profound Arabic salutation is "May your camels never stray."

***

If you're ever in the vicinity of Podunk, Arkansas you should pop into The Road Kill Café. The BLT there, with bear, lichen and toad, is an acquired taste but their possum pie and the raccoon ribs have no equal.

***

A beautiful girl began to work, as a maid, at the village mansion. The Earl explained that one of her chores was to bring the mail to him each day. One day he shouted down "Has the mailman come yet. She replied "No but he's breathing heavy."

***

Most people in America are proud of their home State. However, in Alaska they will tell you that there is positively no place like Nome.

***

VERSE—Auntie Mary had a canary up the leg of her pants but cousin Nile had a crocodile which didn't give him a chance.

***

At a city charity ball the Mayor invited a voluptuous lady to lead off the first dance with him. As they circled the floor, to make small talk, the Mayor said "You are an extraordinary specimen but I have one thing against you." She said "I know, I can feel it."

***

Cricket is often described as the crack of willow on leather. Willow is most upset with her name being taken in vain.

***

What's the difference between a snow man and a snow woman? Snow balls!

***

As a young lad, rooting around in a farmer's field, I found the largest free range duck egg that I had ever seen. It must have been conceived by Moby Duck.

***

The first horse asked the second horse "How did you get on with that young filly zebra last night?" The second horse ruefully replied "Terrible, I wasted the whole night trying to get her pajamas off."

***

In a hay field a mouse was unceremoniously bundled up by a combined harvester. After gnawing her way out, from the bale, she lamented that she had been reaped.

***

A man relocated some two hundred miles away, from home, for a better paying job. He found a new girlfriend and when his old fiance found out she phoned and asked "What has she got that I don't?" He replied "Nothing but she's got it all here."

***

POEM—There was a young woman named Dodd who thought her child came from God. It wasn't the Almighty that lifted her nightie, it was Roger the lodger, the sod.

***

A young man entered a pharmacy and announced "Three French letters, Miss." The elderly female clerk said "Don't you Miss me." He replied "OK, make it four."

***

A new priest knocked on a door in his parish. He commended the family for keeping the catholic tradition with having ten children. The man said "But we aren't catholic" to which the priest replied "Lord take me from this den of iniquity."

***

POEM—There was a man from Devises whose balls were two different sizes. The one was so small, it was no use at all, while the other won fabulous prizes.

***

A golfer went to confession for saying the "F" word during a game. He explained that he hit his ball out of bounds and the priest said "Was it then?" Trying to retrieve his ball a rabbit ran off with it and the priest said "Was it then?" As he got near the rabbit an eagle swooped down and flew off with it ball and all, the priest said "Was it then?" As the eagle soared it was struck by lightning and dropped the rabbit and the ball ended up one foot from the hole. The priest said "Don't tell me you missed the fecking putt."

***

I have sometimes been known to help out with the household laundry. However, it never ceases to amaze me how a woman's discarded clothes invariably end up inside out. This, very issue, is one of the world's most compelling unsolved mysteries.

***

After a lavish cocktail party I sensibly decided to take a taxi home. Good job I did because I encountered a Police DUI sobriety check which thankfully did not involve me. Anyone wanting to take a taxi please contact me as I seem to have one in my garage.

THE END

Made in the USA
Charleston, SC
20 December 2015